Prism of Wounded Light

ASEMANA
BOOKS

Prism of Wounded Light

Poems by:

Amin Haddadi

Translated to English and French from the Persian by Dariush Shahinrad

With twenty-one drawings and paintings by Fatemeh Shakoori

ASEMANA BOOKS

Toronto, Canada
First Edition
© 2025 by Asemana Books

ALL RIGHTS RESERVED.

No part of this book may be reproduced or transmitted in any form or by any means, electronic or mechanical, including photocopying, recording, or by any information storage and retrieval system, without prior written permission from the publisher, except for the inclusion of brief quotations in a review.

Published by ASEMANA BOOKS

ISBN: 9781997503095

Poems by: Amin Haddadi

Translated to English and French from the Persian by: Dariush Shahinrad

Cover illustration & artwork: Fatemeh Shakoori

Book Design: Asemana Books

Cover design: Asemana Books

To find out more about our authors and books visit: www.asemanabooks.ca

ASEMANA
BOOKS

Prism of Wounded Light

The Poet's Note

The poet knows the news. What was I doing all this time? Am I still writing the report even now? I had forgotten to say this: the publisher asked me to write a preface for the book. But I, who find all the pleasure of writing in this very opening encounter with you, of course, I had written to you long before this request. I had *reported* it. Believe me, I never intended to be a reporter of the *night*—not now, when I was becoming the news under bombardment. News disperses; poetry gathers. But news has scattered everyone, my dear. So how can poetry hope to gather "everyone" again? To gather dispersed speech and the word itself? The news was brief: Tehran was bombed! What was I doing all this time? The poet knows the news. So I throw away the earlier draft.

Reporting is futile: "That one" cuts the internet. "This one" gives evacuation warnings. And "they" report the massacre. See? All the pronouns point to *nothing*. On the third night of war, in the desolate beauty and horror of a boulevard in Tehran, I heard a burning angel say: The poet must know the secret. But who even speaks from the pronoun "you"?

اشارهٔ شاعر

شاعر خبر دارد. چه می‌کردم این همه وقت؟ آیا همین حالا هم گزارش می‌نویسم؟ یادم رفته بود این را بگویم. ناشر از من خواسته برای کتاب مقدمه بنویسم. من که تمام عیشِ نوشتن را در همین فتح بابِ آشنایی با تو می‌بینم، معلوم است که خیلی قبل‌تر از این حرف‌ها برایت نوشته بودم. «خبر» داده بودم. باور کن نمی‌خواستم گزارشگرِ شب باشم، آن هم حالا که زیر بمباران داشتم، خبر می‌-شدم. خبر می‌پراکَنَد و شعر گرد می‌آورد: خبر همه را پراکنده است عزیز من. پس چطور شعر می‌خواهد «همه» را جمع کند. کلامِ پراکنده و «کلمه» را جمع کند. خبر کوتاه بود: تهران را زدند! چه می‌کردم این همه وقت؟ شاعر خبر دارد. پس نوشته‌ی قبلی را دور می‌اندازم.

گزارشِ کار بیهوده است: «آن» اینترنت را قطع می‌کند و «این» هشدار تخلیه می‌دهد و «او» گزارشِ کشتار می‌دهد. می‌بینی تمامِ ضمایر به هیچ اشاره می‌کنند. در شب سوم جنگ، در برهوتِ بلواری زیبا و هولناک در تهران شنیدم که فرشته‌ای شعله‌ور می‌-گفت: شاعر باید که راز بداند. راستی چه کسی از ضمیرِ «تو» می‌گوید؟

I know you can speak volumes about the art of *ekphrasis* and offer countless definitions—but the poet brings the news. After all, in the midst of an "evacuation warning," there is no time for theory. The angels of the *Prism of Wounded Light* reveal. The poet knows the secret. And Persian itself is a secret. The verb "neveshtan" (*to write*) in Persian means *ekphrasis*. The poet *writes*. Poetry here *is* writing—a kind of reading of miniatures: one who reads the icon is writing. Ekphrasis—or thinking with images and rendering them in words—in my work, it's like making a wound. Or branding something—with language. But why etch with poetry? Why draw or paint? In the heart of that great social uprising, two forces—two intense emotions—raged within my imagination: Fear and Hope—the courage to create, the sorrow of burning. In both birth and mourning, despite their contrast, there flows a shared force: a desire to cast out, to tear something from one's own body. Not a display of *absence* or a nostalgic "memorial," but an embodiment of absence—a "reminder!" which looks toward the *now*.

The book you are reading is the result of a creative mourning-force. The paintings and sketches opened my mouth, to speak of ancient and scarred icons of today's saints, of fallen angels, and the wounded light. One night in Esfand 1401 (March 2023), in the quiet garden of a small Tehran gallery, I passed through a corridor of

می‌دانم که درباره‌ی هنرِ اکفراسیس می‌توانی حرف‌ها بزنی و تعریف‌های بسیار ارائه کنی اما شاعر خبر می‌دهد. آخر در هنگامه‌ی «هشدار تخلیه» مجالِ حرف نیست. فرشتگانِ «منشورِ زخم نور» افشا می‌کنند. شاعر راز می‌داند؛ و فارسی راز است. فعلِ «نگاشتن» در فارسی یعنی اکفراسیس. شاعر می‌نگارد. شاعری اینجا نگاشتن است. یک‌جور مینیاتورخوانی است: او که تمثال می‌خواند، دارد می‌نگارد. اکفراسیس یا همان اندیشیدن به‌- مددِ تصویر و تصویر را نگاشتن؛ در کارِ من، مثل زخم زدن است یا چیزی را داغ کردنِ آن هم با کلمه. اما چرا طرح زدن با شعر؟ چرا طراحی و نقاشی؟ در کورانِ آن جنبشِ عظیم، دو نیرو، دو احساسِ شدید در خیالِ من بیداد می‌کرد؛ بیم و امید: شجاعتِ ساختن و سوگِ سوختن. در زایش و سوگ به‌رغمِ تضاد، یک نیروی مشترک، جریان دارد: میل به برون‌افکندن، میل به چیزی از تنِ خود کَندن. نه نمایشِ نیستی و «یادبود» که گذشته‌نگر است بلکه به غیاب و فقدان تن‌بخشیدن و «یادآر!» که رو به اکنون دارد.

کتابی که می‌خوانی حاصلِ نیروی سوگِ آفرینش‌گرانه است. تابلوها و طرح‌ها زبانِ مرا باز کردند تا از تمثالِ باستانی و مخدوشِ قدیسانِ امروز، از فرشتگانِ مطرود و زخمِ نور بنویسم. شبی در اسفند ۱۴۰۱ در باغِ کوچک گالریِ خلوت در تهران از دهلیزِ سوگ گذشتم و حالا در هراسِ موشک‌بارانِ جنگ (۱۴۰۴) دارم به این کتیبه‌ی بیم و امید نگاه می‌کنم. به شعله‌ی این شمع.

mourning. Now, in the terror of wartime missile strikes (1404 / 2025), I gaze upon this tablet of fear and hope—this candle's flame. How naked the flame is! Do you see? Let me tell you frankly what I hold in my heart: in all the poems in this book, the image of a naked candle flame flares in my mind—the source of its light: a historical wound, now like a prism before your eyes, like a mirror before the beloved, warming my face. I know the poet may be killed in captivity, like *Baktash*, or might die from the impact of a sudden, midnight bombardment. But poetry remains witness. The homeland—this naked candle, this burning cypress—remains witness to its slain.

Let it not go unspoken: in my other works, I've always been "alone." But this book is the product of collective poetry. What you read may arise from the impossibility of translation—the very idea of the untranslatable nature of poetry. This is no longer a question of *translation*—but of a prism. The poems have not been translated, rather, they are being composed, moment by moment, in other forms. Thus, each is a thing of its own—yet in other languages, sometimes they take visual form, sometimes they speak to readers in three tongues of poetry: Persian, English, and French. Still, something always remains unsaid in between—a light that cannot be published. The secret of the prism is this:

چقدر برهنه است شعله‌ی شمع! می‌بینی؟ بگذار آنچه در دل دارم با تو فاش بگویم: در تمامی شعرهای این کتاب، خیالِ برهنگیِ شعله‌ی یک شمع زبانه می‌کشد. سرچشمه‌ی روشنایی یک زخمِ تاریخی که اکنون همچو منشوری پیشِ‌رویت، همچو آینه‌ای برابر معشوق، چهره‌ی مرا گرم می‌کند. می‌دانم ممکن است شاعر در بند کشته شود یا به اشارتِ بمبارانی شبانه و نابهنگام بمیرد اما «شعر» شاهد می‌ماند. وطن، این شمعِ برهنه، این سروِ شعله‌ور، شاهدِ کُشتگانِ خویش می‌ماند.

ناگفته نماند که در آثارِ دیگرم، همواره «تنها» بوده‌ام اما این کتاب ماحصلِ شعری جمعی است. شاید آنچه می‌خوانی از سرِ ناممکنیِ برگردان و ایده‌ی ترجمه‌ناپذیریِ شعر پریده باشد. دیگر حرف بر سر ترجمه نیست که «منشور» است. شعرها ترجمه نشده‌اند بلکه دم‌به‌دم به بیان‌های دیگر سروده می‌شوند. این است که هر کدام یک چیزند اما با زبان‌های دیگر گاه به تصویر درمی‌آیند و گاه با خوانندگانِ سه زبانِ شعرباره [فارسی، انگلیسی، فرانسه] سخن می‌گویند. با این همه همیشه چیزی این وسط ناگفته می‌ماند. نوری منتشرناشدنی؛ رازِ «منشور» در این است:

> Even if in art and poetry's craft
> None but you may dare rise in pride,
> Your own virtues, you cannot say in verse—
> Your own image, you cannot draw.
> — *Kasa'i Marvazi*

Amin Hadadi
Tehran, Summer 2025

هرچند در صناعتِ نقشِ و علوم شعر
جز مر تو را روا نبود سرفراشتن
اوصافِ خویشتن نتوانی به شعر گفت
تمثالِ خویشتن نتوانی نگاشتن

«کسایی مروزی»

امین حدادی
تهران/ تابستانِ ١٤٠٤

I

چهره‌ی ابری سیاه در باد

رؤیای طفلی تب‌دار

جنینی در رَحِمِ شب

یا پرنده‌ای کوچک در گردابِ آب‌های دوردست

حرفی نیست!

می‌توانم «تو» باشم

اگر گوش بِسپاری به دیدنِ من.

The countenance of a black cloud in wind

The dream of a fevered child

An embryo in the uterus of night

Or a small bird in the whirlpool of distant waters

No worries!

I can be "you"

If you lend an ear to seeing me.

Le visage d'un nuage noir au vent

Le songe d'un enfant fiévreux,

Un embryon dans l'utérus de la nuit

Ou un petit oiseau dans le tourbillon des eaux lointaines

Aucun problème !

Je peux être « toi »

Si tu donnes de l'oreille à me voir.

II

شب‌باره‌ها

خفاش‌های مُقرّب

عفریشتگانِ هوا

به چلّه‌ی طفلِ نورخواره‌ی من

ـ مرگ ـ

چه گریان می‌رقصند:

بال در بال

کیفور در سوگِ سپیده‌دم

به دعوتِ تاریکی.

The nuctanderers

The devoted bats

The witchgels of air and lust

How weeping they dance

To the quarantine of my lightfed child

-Death-

Wing in wing

Rapturous in the mourn of mourning

To the invitation of darkness.

Les noctambules

Les chauves-souris séraphiques

Les gorganges de l'air et de l'ardeur

Comme elles pleurent en dansant

Lors de la quarantaine de mon enfant jourisson

-la mort-

Aile dans l'aile

Joviales au deuil du matin

À l'invitation de l'obscurité.

III

متبرّک باد زندگی!

حالا که در جشنِ سایه‌ها

مریمی دیگر

پرده برمی‌دارد از مرگ

با لبخندِ دخترش عیسی.

Blessed be life

Now that in the feast of shadows

Another Marie

Tears away the hymen of death

With the smile of her daughter, Jesus!

Bénie soit la vie

Maintenant qu'à la fête des ombres

Une autre Marie

Déchire l'hymen de la mort

Au sourire de sa fille, Jésus !

IV

چهره‌ها که در هم می‌آمیزند
تن معنایی دیگر می‌گیرد
دور و نزدیک
مثل سایه
که خواهشِ نور است از تاریکی.

آن‌سو
چشمِ ماه
شرمِ خوشِ عشق را ببین!
چه برقی می‌زند
در شب‌زنده‌داریِ اشباح.

When the faces are mingled

The body finds another meaning

Far and close

Like shadow

Which is the imploration of light from darkness.

Look on the other side

The eye of the moon

The happy shame of love!

How it sparkles

At the vigil of the phantoms.

Lorsque les visages s'entremêlent

Le corps prend un autre sens

Loin et proche

Comme l'ombre

Qui est l'imploration de la lumière à l'obscurité.

Vois à l'autre côté

L'œil de la lune

La vergogne douce de l'amour !

Comme elle brille

À la veillée des fantômes.

V

نه روبند و
نقاب
نه سیماچه و
چشم‌بند
ای شبِ منحط
اکنون چهره برمی‌دارم
تا بمیری
از فرطِ روشنی.

Neither veil,

Nor mask;

Neither persona,

Nor blindfold;

O decadent night!

Now I take off the face

So that you die

By excess of brightness.

Ni voile,

Ni masque ;

Ni effigie,

Ni bandeau ;

Ô décadente nuit !

Je dé-face maintenant mon visage

Pour que tu meures

À force de l'éclat.

VI

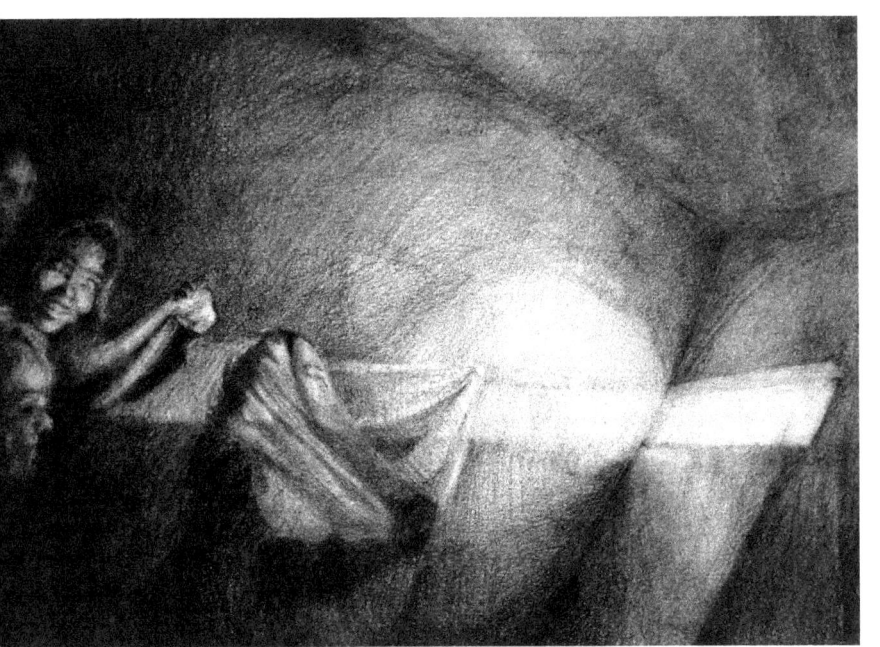

گاه تابوتِ نوری بر دوش و بیگاه

مثل خوابِ گهواره‌ای بر رود

بنگر

این طفلِ بیمار را!

که چه آرام

بَر سَرِ دست می‌بَرند

مادرانِ بیداری.

Sometimes a coffin of light on the shoulders;

Other times,

Like the sleep of a cradle on the river;

Look

At this sick child!

How calmly

The mothers of wakefulness

Carry him on their hands.

Tantôt un cercueil de lumière sur les épaules ;

Tantôt,

Comme le sommeil d'un berceau sur le fleuve ;

Regarde

Cet enfant infirme !

Que bénignement

Le portent à la main

Les mères de l'éveil.

VII

نگاه کن

زخمِ آن نورِ نورسیده

چه رعشه‌ی خوشی انداخته بر اندامِ فرشتگانِ پاییز

و چه سرودی می‌خوانند

از نامِ زیباترین رفتگانِ این سال

می‌شنوی؟

Look!

What a happy quiver has sent

The wound of that recently-arrived light

Down the body of the angels of autumn;

And what hymn they chant

Of the name of the most beautiful bygones of this year;

Do you hear?

Regarde !

La blessure de cette lumière nouveau-venue,

Quel doux frisson a-t-elle envoyé dans le corps des anges d'automne ;

Et quel hymne ils chantent

Du nom des départis les plus beaux de cette année ;

Tu entends?

VIII

نیم‌رخم در نور

چشم به صدایی از دور

به نجوایی مرا می‌بینی

تنها ـ

کو دستی که بگیری؟

My profile in the light

Looking forward to a sound from far away

You see me in a whisper

Alone-

Where is a hand that you take?

Mon profil dans la lumière

Guettant une voix du loin

Tu me vois par un murmure

Seul-

Où est une main que tu prends ?

IX

نادیدنی اما

تماشایی‌ست

آرایشِ اشباح:

در کُنج‌های مَحشر و

گوشه‌های روشنِ شهر.

It's invisible,

But spectacular:

The array of the phantoms

In the apocalyptic corners

And bright angles of the city.

C'est invisible,

Mais spectaculaire :

L'arrangement des fantômes

Aux coins apocalyptiques,

Aux angles limpides de la ville.

X

از پنجره خونی زرد می‌آید

به درون می‌ریزد   رودی روشن

و حلقه می‌زند دورِ گردن   آوازی از روز

زیبایی وحشتناک توانِ عشرت

می‌بینی؟

گاه نور، کور می‌کند.

Through the window comes a yellow blood

Pours in   a bright river

And encircles the neck   a song of day

Terrible beauty   ability to enjoy

Do you see?

Sometimes the light,   blinds!

Vient par la fenêtre un sang jaune

Se déverse dedans   un fleuve limpide

Et cerne le cou   un chant du jour

Beauté terrible   puissance de jouissance

Tu vois ?

Parfois la lumière   aveugle !

XI

در سورِ سایه‌ها

هزار سر و یک سودا:

«هر فرشته‌ای هراس‌انگیز است».

In the feast of shadows,

A thousand heads and one ambition:

« Ein jeder Engel ist schrecklich ».

À la fête des ombres,

Mille têtes et une seule ambition ;

« Ein jeder Engel ist schrecklich ».

XII

در خلسه‌ای ناب

زیرِ دوشِ نور

سیاه‌پوش اما عریان‌تر از روز

سایه‌های محبوب و جن‌زده

مادرانِ اضطراب را فرامی‌خوانم

این‌بار

به پیشوازِ زخمِ نور.

In pure ecstasy,

Under the shower of light,

Dressed in black but   more naked than day;

I conjure the beloved and possessed shadows,

The mothers of anxiety;

This time,

Going out to meet the wound of light.

Dans une extase pure,

Sous la douche de lumière,

Vêtues en noir, mais   plus nues que le jour ;

Je conjure les ombres favorites et possédées,

Les mères de l'anxiété ;

Cette fois,

À l'accueil de la blessure de lumière.

XIII

تنها شعله‌ای می‌توانست

دهانِ تو را زیبا کند

و صدای معطّرِ خنده‌ات را

سرودِ این زندگی دهشت‌ناک.

ای فرشته‌ی کوچکِ ظلمت!

تنها شعله‌ای می‌توانست

بهانه کند

روز میلاد تو را

برای یک شب‌نشینیِ بی‌پایان.

Only a flame could have

Beautified your mouth;

And the hymn of this dreadful life,

The perfumed timbre of your laugh.

O small angel of darkness!

Only a flame could have

Given the day of your birth

As an excuse for

An interminable soiree.

Seulement une flamme aurait pu

Enjoliver ta bouche ;

Et le timbre parfumé de ton rire,

L'hymne de cette vie effrayante.

Ô petit ange de l'obscurité !

Seulement une flamme aurait pu

Prétexter

Du jour de ta naissance

Pour une soirée interminable.

XIV

ردای نورْ بر دوش

از سوگ می‌آیی

که چنین زیبا

خیره‌ای به خاک

ای ارواحِ سیه‌پوش

دخترانِ نورسیده‌ی زمان

کجا می‌بَرید

چهره‌های روشنِ سالیانِ مرا؟

Having shouldered a robe of light,

You come from mourning

You are staring at the soil

So graciously.

O spirits dressed in black!

Recently arrived daughters of time!

Whereto are you taking

The bright visages of my years?

La robe de lumière au dos,

Tu viens des funérailles

Que si joliment

Tu fixes le sol.

Ô âmes vêtues de noir !

Les filles du temps nouvellement arrivées !

Où portez-vous

Les visages lumineux de mes années ?

XV

در واپسین ساعات روز

از سایه‌ام کنده می‌شوم

مثل برگی   از گُلبرگ

و به وقتِ گرگ‌ومیش

از سایه‌ام عبور می‌دهم

خیالِ فصل‌های نیامده را.

In the latest hours of the day,

I'm detached from my shadow

Like a leaf from the petal;

And, in the twilight,

I pass through my shadow

The image of unarrived seasons.

Aux dernières heures de la journée,

Je me détache de mon ombre

Comme une feuille   du pétale ;

Et, au moment du crépuscule,

Je fais passer à travers mon ombre

L'image des saisons non-arrivées.

XVI

چه لذتی‌ست در عبور تاریکی

از دریچه‌ها و

آنسوی آینه‌ها

و لمسِ نور

به وقتِ عیشِ مدام.

What a joy there is in the passage of darkness

Through the vents and

On the other side of mirrors,

And in the touching of light

In the hour of perpetual orgy.

Quelle joie dans le passage de l'obscurité

À travers les soupiraux et

À l'autre côté des miroirs,

En touchant la lumière

Lors de l'orgie perpétuelle.

XVII

بر بالینِ روزهای بلند

نور

آخرین مهمانِ ناخوانده‌ی زندگی‌ست:

بر بالین من گریه مکن

برقص!

بگذار مرگ

نورافشانی کند   میانِ این همه رنگ.

At the bedside of long days,

The light

Is the last uninvited guest of life.

Do not weep at my bedside;

Dance!

Let death

Gleam   through these colors.

Au chevet des longs jours,

La lumière

Est la dernière intruse de la vie.

Ne pleure pas à mon chevet ;

Danse !

Laisse la mort

Briller au sein de ces couleurs.

XVIII

ریشه‌ها برآمده از خاک

رقصِ شبح،   سایه کشیده بر دیوار

پنجه‌های ارواح، برخاسته به دعا از وحشت

و دستانِ ما

که فوج فوج بازمی‌گردند

گشوده اما

بی‌پَر.

The roots sprouted from the soil,

The dance of fantom, having cast a shadow on the wall,

The claws of the spirits raised in prayer of terror,

And our hands

Who return in large groups;

Open, but,

Wingless.

Les racines jaillies du sol,

La danse du fantôme, ombrageant le mur,

Les griffes des esprits levées en priant de terreur,

Et nos mains

Qui retournent en groupes,

Ouvertes, mais,

Sans ailes.

XIX

در هاله‌ای سپید
با چهره‌های بسیار می‌آید
و با هزاران حرف
در چشمی پنهان می‌شود.

It comes in a white halo,

With many faces;

And, with thousands of words,

It hides in an eye.

Il vient, entouré d'un halo blanc,

Avec beaucoup de visages ;

Et, avec des milliers de paroles,

Se cache dans un œil.

XX

نه نور و نه کلمه

در آغاز، کار بود

گوته می‌گفت.

عجب نیست

حالا که کار به پایان رسیده

سایه‌ها با او از آغاز می‌پرسند؟!

Neither light nor word

In the beginning, there was work-

Goethe used to say.

Isn't it strange that,

Now that the work is finished,

The shadows should ask it about the beginning?

Ni lumière, ni Verbe ;

Au commencement était le travail -

Disait Goethe.

N'est-il pas étrange que,

Maintenant que le travail est terminé,

Les ombres le questionnent sur le passé !?

XXI

صورت‌ها

در سایه‌روشنِ نور زیبایند

یا چیزها و اشیاء

زیرِ نورِ چهره‌ها؟

هیچ‌کس نمی‌داند

جز سایه‌ی صورتِ تو

بر کاسه‌ی روشنِ آب.

Is it the faces

That are beautiful in the chiaroscuro of light

Or things and objects

Under the light of the faces?

Nobody knows,

Except the shadow of your face upon the bright bowl of water.

Ce sont les figures

Qui sont belles à claire-obscure de la lumière,

Ou bien les choses et les objets

Sous la lumière des visages ?

Personne ne sait,

Sauf l'ombre de ta figure sur le clair bol d'eau.

Behind the words & images

Amin Haddadi (born September 1992) is a poet, translator, and literary critic based in Tehran. His published works include "Open Wounds and Tehran Spleen" (2021, Afraz Publishing); "Lathe Working the Metal of the Future: Four Fragments and an Anthology of Portraits by Majid Naficy" (2019, Baru Publishing); "The Entrance Permission Cycle: Pilgrimage Prayers for Fear and Wandering in Non-Place" (2023, Baru Publishing); and "Dialogue with the Germen: A Suit with Two Unfinished Letters" (2025, Beyraqhā va Lakkehā).

His latest poetry book, "Prism of Wounded Light," a trilingual edition of poems accompanied by twenty-one drawings and paintings, has been published by Asemana Books. Several of his articles and translations have appeared in literary journals in Iran and abroad, both in print and online.

Haddadi holds a degree in cognitive psychology and works in psychotherapy, alongside engaging in projects in the field of art therapy.

Fatemeh Shakouri is an Iranian artist born in 1979 in Tehran. She earned her bachelor's degree in fashion design from the Tehran University of Art and her master's degree in art research from Allameh Tabataba'i University. At the age of 19, she became an art teacher, a role that significantly influenced her work and for which she has received prestigious national awards in the field of art education. Shakouri has held three solo exhibitions and participated in over 40 group exhibitions. She currently lives and works in Tehran. The present collection was exhibited in March 2023 under the title *"In Praise of Light"* at Doost Gallery in Tehran.

Dariush Shahinrad (born October 1997) holds a degree in Pure Mathematics from Sharif University of Technology and a Ph.D. in French Language and Literature from the University of Tehran. He is engaged in translating literary and philosophical texts and books from French and English. His doctoral dissertation focuses on Espacementale Poetry movement (sheʻr-i ḥajm), the Other Poetry movement (*Sheʻr-e Digar*), and Bijan Elahi, modernist Persian poet. He has published articles in Iran, and several of his translations and books are currently in press.

Asemana Books

Devoted to Publishing Diasporic, Underrepresented and Progressive Literature on the Middle East.

Email: Asemanabooks@gmail.com

Webpage: asemanabooks.ca

Scholarly and Academic Research

- *Tanglusha of a Thousand Images: Essays on Culture and Literature* – Reza Farokhfal – 2024
- *Language, People, and Society: Iranian Minority Languages and Literary Traditions* – Edited by Amir Kalan, Mahdi Ganjavi, Anisa Jafari, Lale Javanshir – 2024
- *Music on the Borderland: Remembering and Chronicling the 1979 Revolution's Shadow on Iranian Music* – Keyan Emami – 2024
- *Implications of Class Analysis in Capitalist Imperialism* – Mohammad Hajinia and Shahrzad Mojab – 2024
- *Dark Night and Phoenixes of the Ashes: Nima Yushij's Poetry from 1932–1942* – Ramin Ahmadi – 2024
- *Whispers of Oasis: Likoo's Poetic Mirage* – Mahdi Ganjavi, Amin Fatemi, Mansour Alimoradi – 2024
- *Hafez and Irony* – Reza Farokhfal – 2024

- *Kurdish Women at the Core of the Historical Contradictions on Feminism and Nationalism* – Shahrzad Mojab – 2023
- *The Peasant Uprising of Mukriyan 1952–1953: Consulate Documents, Diplomatic Correspondence, and the Press Coverage* – Amir Hassanpour – 2022

Critical Edition

- *The History of Changes in Iran* – Mirza Agha Khan Kermani, edited by M. Rezaei Tazik – 2024
- *Rostam in the Twenty-Second Century* – Abdulhussain San'atizadeh Kermani, edited by Mahdi Ganjavi and M. Mansouri – 2017

Poetry

- *Shape of Extinction* – Poetry of Bijan Jalali, Translated by Adeeba Shahid Talukder and Aria Fani - 2025
- *One Hundred Nights of Yearning* – Mansour Noorbakhsh – 2025
- *Songs of Barbad* – Amir Hakimi – 2024
- *With My Shadows, I Created Myself* – Hadi Ebrahimi Roudbaraki - 2024
- *Citizens of September* – Saeid Rezadoust - 2024

- *Wonder of Memory* – Amir Hakimi – 2023
- *Galaxy Has No Memory of the Sunset* – Mahdi Ganjavi – 2023
- *Strangers Who Live in Me* – Mahdi Ganjavi – 2021
- *Exiled to the Rocky* – Ali Fatolahi – 2018

Fiction & Plays

- *Escape from the Girl's Complex* _ Mahbobe Mousavi – 2025
- *Yousef, Joseph, Guiseppe* – Ali Foumani - 2025
- *An Iranian Odyssey* – Rana Soleimani – 2025
- *Lead to Evil* – Javad Alavi – 2025
- *We Are Drunk and Broken, and No One Is Witnessing Us* – Mahdi Ganjavi – 2025
- *Someone Had Died in Front of Our House* – Akbar Falahzadeh – 2024
- *Zinat* – Vahid Zarrabi Nasab – 2024
- *Siberian Crane* – Ali Foumani - 2024
- *Elephants Reached the Plain* – Kaveh Oveisi - 2024
- *Textual Mosaic* – Marzieh Sotoudeh – 2024
- *Expectations of a Dream* – Mahdi Ganjavi – 2020

Prisme de Blessure de Lumière

Poèmes par:
Amin Haddadi

Traduction de Dariush Shahinrad

Avec vingt et un dessins et tableaux de Fatemeh Shakoori

منشورِ زخمِ نور

امین حدادی

ترجمهٔ فرانسه و انگلیسی
داریوش شاهین‌راد

همراه با بیست‌ویک طراحی و نقاشی از فاطمه شکوری

Asemana Books is devoted to publishing diasporic, underrepresented, and progressive literature on the Middle East.

asemanabooks.ca

ASEMANA BOOKS

www.ingramcontent.com/pod-product-compliance
Lightning Source LLC
Chambersburg PA
CBHW071223160426
43196CB00012B/2400